THE INHERITANCE

POEMS AND PHOTOGRAPHS

JUSTIN HAMM

ಞ

BLUE HORSE PRESS REDONDO BEACH, CALIFORNIA 2019

THE INHERITANCE

POEMS AND PHOTOGRAPHS

JUSTIN HAMM

Blue Horse Press
318 Avenue I # 760
Redondo Beach,
California 90277

Copyright © 2019 by Justin Hamm
All rights reserved
Printed in the United States of America

Cover photo: "Inheritance." Justin Hamm ©
Used by permission

Editors: Jeffrey and Tobi Alfier
Blue Horse Press logo: Amy Lynn Hayes (1996)

ISBN 978-0-578-50548-0

No part of this book may be reproduced or transmitted in any form or by any means, electronic or mechanical, including photocopy, recording, or any information storage and retrieval system now known or to be invented, without permission in writing from the publisher, except by a reviewer who wishes to quote brief passages in connection with a review written for inclusion in a magazine, newspaper or broadcast.

FIRST EDITION © 2019

This and other Blue Horse Press Titles may be found at
www.bluehorsepress.com

For Leta. The legacy of your example enriches us all

Acknowledgments

"Sleeping in the Town of My Birth," *Euphony*
"After the Argument," "Pelicans," and "Hovland, Minnesota," *Up North Lit*
"Colorado," *Light: A Journal of Poetry and Photography*
"Tribute," *The Tower Journal*
"Don't want much—," *Stoneboat*
"Ohio County, Kentucky, 1985," *Ghost City Review*
"The Pilgrim," *New Reader Magazine*
"The Inheritance" and "Storm, Rural Missouri," *Escape Into Life*

Contents

POEMS

1. *Don't want much—*
2. *I Will Tell You Where I've Been*
4. *Ohio County, Kentucky, 1985*
8. *The Carpenter*
10. *Sometimes, in the good old films,*
12. *Stranger at the Only Fueling Station in Kingston, Arkansas*
14. *Three Stanzas Ending With God*
16. *The Pilgrim*
18. *Tribute*
19. *Sleeping in the Town of My Birth*
21. *Panic Attack*
23. *After the Argument*
26. *Pelicans*
27. *Federico Garcia Lorca Blues*
28. *A Moment in Kansas*
29. *The Inheritance*
35. *Hovland, Minnesota*
37. *The most we can hope for*
39. *Storm, Rural Missouri*
40. *Colorado*

PHOTOGRAPHS

43. *The Work Glove*
44. *Tiny Tilted Cross*
45. *Sunlight on the Tracks*
46. *Harvested*
47. *Among the Wildflowers*
48. *Reclamation Project*

49. *Barn, First Snow*
50. *The Abandoned Silo*
51. *The Corn Crib*
52. *Uneven Track*
53. *Tenor Guitar, Barn Wood Loft*
54. *No Trespassing*
55. *The Windmill*
56. *For Sale #3*

About the Author

Poems

Don't want much—

just to write one little poem, sharp
as obsidian, to snake-charm time
and preacher-heal cynicism,
to build a ladder to the distant stars
and live two-thousand eighty-six years
in the hearts of Danish schoolchildren
deep in the belly of the immortal raven.

I Will Tell You Where I've Been

Look off in the direction
the weathervane points,
past the place where rain
raps sideways against the silo,
a stranger touching
the shoulder of a stranger
before asking permission to pass.

Look beyond the chrome plant.
It gleams like a future metropolis,
crying out corn steam
white as the teeth
of the pastor's eldest son.

There, where warped-wood trestles
teeter over wildflower prairie
seasoned with primrose, goatsbeard,
sneezeweed and bristly buttercup—
that is the place I have been.

I went to walk along the banks
of the muddy creek, though I should
have known better. My heart is still
my heart, and I have not prayed
in earnest since I was a child.

Would you believe me if I swore
I only go there after a downpour?
That is when you can hear her rushing,
bubbling up. Sobbing, like my mother,
for all the children she's swallowed
in the holy name of love.

Ohio County, Kentucky, 1985

1.

I stand in our
ancestor's field
all of Kentucky
a green inferno
at my back

I stand there in
one shoe
Grandmother trying
goddamnit
to get ahold of me
so as to spit shine
my filthy face

Grandfather picks through
the warped-wood barn
for his history
before the coal company
has its way

The air in this place
is ripe
with some kind
of weather

2.

They called my grandfather's
grandfather The Preacher
and that is what
he was

This land was his land

He rode these backhills
in his black coat
carrying the hidden ear
of judgement
close to his heart

His whip they say
he kept down inside
his saddlebag

I see him that afternoon
me as I told you
in his field
in my one shoe
don't ask me how

and when
the corpse of him
opens its vast red mouth
the crows pour out
like the shadows
of a thousand diamonds

3.

All around us
the insects whine

All around us
Kentucky like one
great green blaze
of summer

Grandmother closes in
reaches for the sleeve
of my t-shirt

I see the dead man
out there on his mount

I hear him speak
the bodies of those
dark birds

I know the family
secrets

I know all of them

The skies now
the color of healing
bruises

I look up
into Grandmother's
horse-wild eyes

I let her catch me

The Carpenter

Sawdust drifted
against his bootsoles

Fingers calloused,
palms ghosted white
with drywall mud

Who knows vibration
of circular saw
and router

Who knows
the hieroglyphs
of practical geometry

Whose pencil pins
stray hairs
behind his ear

Who also grasps
the cold algorithms
of construction

The utter violence
in his tools

The slicing
and the striking

The ripping
and the binding

All necessary
to build or repair

This knowledge
too
lives quietly
in his hands

Sometimes, in the good old films,

wrenches turn
and on roll
the eighteen wheelers.
And people
still make love
to their cigarettes.

This poem is for
the men whose fathers'
tool belts have been taken.

They stare
from tattered recliners
through beer-blurred eyes
down cinematic highways
that seem
to stretch on forever,
much like unemployment.
Eventually they begin
to wonder whether
sun-baked asphalt
might make
a decent bed.

This poem is for
those men.
And it comes with
a can of Coors

Stranger at the Only Fueling Station in Kingston, Arkansas

He's a songwriter, he tells us.
Used to sleep in Nashville, Tennessee.
Now he keeps a ranch up over
that middle mountain.

Says he wrote quite a few
of John Denver's early songs
under a different man's name,
which I know isn't true,
but there is no doubting
the whiskey barrels of grief
behind his wide, yellow eyes.

My wife is passed six months, he tells us.
When the nine angels come
to claim my bones too
I traded them my front two teeth
for a little more time
to make up words in the dark.

Cigarette smoke leaks
from that very toothgap
as he laughs his bullfrog laugh
and makes a guitar gesture
down around his hips.
Then his face slackens, lips
beginning to lightly tremble.

They come from the mountain, he says.
Their faces cold as the moon's.
I wasn't ready for them, he says.
Jesus, he says, I was still sweeping
her hair from the corners of our room.

Three Stanzas Ending With God

    1.

Through a ragged church's
single-window eye,
miles of narrow highway
strangled in weed and vine.
Here you could pursue
a whisper for centuries
backward or forward—
either leads directly
to the icy lips of God.

    2.

The adjacent field:
two barns teeter and tilt
away from one another
like jealous siblings
trapped too long inside
the same car or family.
If the first ever decides
to shove the second over,
this is but one more way
we might make measure
of the swirling moods of God.

3.

The heron leaps off the page
of the Chinese poem
and glides into my own,
a broken corpse-snake
dangling from his bill.
What else can this be
but another love ballad
about the clandestine
arrangements of God?

The Pilgrim

Sunset pours into the shattered eyes
of an old farmhouse.
Out front the gravel road bends
around someone else's corn.

A man, burnt red from outdoor labor,
wipes his hands over the belly
of his denim shirt, discovers there
an oily spring oozing from his palms.

The man looks and looks and finally finds
the spot they buried the stillborn—
up near the house, as she'd insisted, so she
could watch the grave from the sitting room.

This: a private affair. The crows above,
in their funeral best, mind their manners,
and the deer dare not creep closer
than the edge of the Hickory wood.

The man kneels near a smooth rock.

When it happened, he took it badly,
refused an equal share in the burden.
There's no making that up to her now.
But he can finally set free some words
he has shouldered these ten-thousand days.

They are good words, but insufficient.
He is grateful, at least, to deliver them
before the mortician picks his pockets
and paints away the craters around
his own window-broken eyes.

Tribute

Go down and tell
them who works
in the lower valley:
the great mother
claims seven fat oxen.
The loggers must numb
their rebel tongues.

Sleeping in the Town of My Birth

is not particularly a comfort
nor an anxiety
most of the time.

Surrounded by the usual joys,
my daughters and wife
snoring beside me,
a third child about the size
of a blueberry in the belly,
the usual worries nonetheless
flash like slasher movie scenes
against my closed eyelids.
Rare cancers, car crashes,
humiliating professional rejections.

And stranger things, too.
Old blues riffs ringing like
invisible church bells.
Something Jim once said
to Huck in the Good Book.

The only real difference here
is the nagging knowledge
that somewhere among
the giant warped Victorians
a man sleeps better than I—
the man who sold to my mother
the Fentanyl patches
she tore open with her teeth
and animal-lapped with her tongue
until her damaged heart went quiet
one bone-numb winter night
as my father dreamed
his last hopeful dreams
of ever growing happy
beside her.

I am a gentle person, ask around.
I strum a ukulele; I read
to kindergarteners professionally.
But I confess, when not at my best,
I've imagined entering
his bedroom, silent as he snores.
Of covering his eyes, plugging his nose
with thumb and finger,
and pouring her ashes thick
into his gaping mouth-hole,
so he too can know firsthand
the pain of waking at three AM
choking on her memory.

Panic Attack

is what my doctor calls it
when my mind and body
get a twenty-minute divorce,
one continuing to raise the children,
albeit shakily,
while the other flails and thrashes
like some animal
caught in the hunter's rusty trap—
leftovers, of course,
from time out of mind,
the age of constant fight or flight,
but also from a childhood
where flying dishes, police sirens,
and pulled-knife threats
might slice through the silence
of any given midnight.

The savior in this situation
is tiny and pink
and should be taken once daily
with food.

She is a decent god, as gods go,
her tribute merely the top
end of my emotions.
I can live, I tell myself,
with this tempered joy.
I don't have to cry every time
my daughters paint
a three-eyed elephant
or a Starburst sunset.

The worst part? Once, a fine
hermit lived inside me.
Every time I swallow, a few more
of his beard hairs fall out,
scattering to the four winds.
If you look closely into my eyes,
you can still see him
staring out at the world,
processing, in quiet confusion,
from behind the dimmed bulbs
of my medication eyes.

After the Argument

1.

Everyone you love
sleeps in a quiet room of midnight.
Which is of some comfort,
at least.

2.

Alone with the words
you should not have said,
you rest your head
against the storm door,
trying to tame your breath.

In the neighbors' window,
pink and green lights,
the Aurora Borealis
of a television talent show
strobing in the darkness.

A gruff-voiced dog
barks his ineloquent warning
to the coyotes in the field
behind the house.

3.

An uninvited memory:
your mother and father
embrace in a dingy kitchen,
just an hour or so after
she held a serrated knife
to the white of his throat.

In a corner, you
and your baby sister huddle
like broken puppies,
trying to tame the violence
of your sobs.

4.

The moon a round bone
afloat in a black lake.
Time, a knife. Memory, a knife.
Our failures to understand one another—
small blades, every one.

You tell yourself you are better
than what you come from.

You tell yourself that every
couple has it out now and then.

You look up toward
the neighbors' house again.

Christ, you think, there is
no loneliness on earth
like watching someone
watch someone else
try to dance.

Pelicans

A pouch of white pelicans
on the ancient Mississippi,
a hundred or so sailing
delicately over the bones
of sunken steamboats
and their forever-grinning pilots.

I crouch near the river bank,
stare through a cloud of awe
despite the cool April mist.

How strange—to make such fuss
over a creature I've read
would gladly swallow the teeth
from my children's skulls.

I admit it. Something dark
has hunted me a long time now.
No one can see it, but I can
see it, just as I can see the songs
that crawl from a widow's eyes.

Federico Garcia Lorca Blues

These blues are lunar, blues of the moon
and the moonlight and the white spell
the moonlight casts on tree-stubbled hills.

They belong to Andalusia, yet I have seen them too
folk dancing the streets of Chicago in a gale
and smelled them over the insulin bottle

my grandfather tilted every evening
before needling out the potion
that staved off the duke of all shadows.

These are blues that incubate in the eager
throats of scavenger birds latched
to the abandoned silos of the Ozarks.

But most of all, they are the blues of the four
varieties of human sleep—three of them defined,
the fourth still to be discovered.

A Moment in Kansas

Somewhere in Kansas
a night train torches
through the dark stomach
of the prairie.

The man in the car
on the rural route
turns his head
for just a moment
and wonders if
he has ever made
his father proud.

But only a moment.
Now he turns from
the disembodied flames.
At the crossroad
he signals left.
The engine hums
the ballad of whatever
comes after.

The Inheritance

   1.

There is a photo
of you
in our first few
years together
when we lived
in the woods
and shared meat
with the neighbors

You cradled
a pumpkin
in both arms
like an infant

Your eyes then
were so bright

   2.

My mother
had an instinct
for violence

Over the years
I learned
which words
would cause
the cold sting
of her hand
across my face

Then I said them
and said them
just to punish her
with guilt

   3.

I was five
when my grandfather
took me out
to the farm
where his brother
slung hay
and led me around
on that
starkissed beauty
of a horse

Grandpa was so
gentle with me
and with the mare
who seemed half
in love
from the way she
nuzzled his hair

and yet

who do you think
taught my mother
to hit?

   4.

If I loved you once
for those
bright eyes
I love you more now
for everything
that has made them
a little tired

This is a story
about how
a cycle breaks
about how you
taught me
there are better rivers
in which we can
drown
our ancestors' rage

This is a story
about our confident
daughters
who know nothing
of pain except
the hairbrush through
tough tangles
before bed

As for me—
I know nothing
of what you have
borne
to get us here

But listen: I am
trying

5.

Green fingers
of grass
reach up through late
April snow

A good man
we know
lies unconscious
in the hospital
with a stroke

Our new baby
would have been
about a month old
by now

We walk
the gaudy aisles
of the super center
my hand against
the small of
your back

Our girls alternate
requests for all things
sugar
with questions
about the nature
of God

Here we are

We have
done it

We have
made it

It feels so much
like coming home
when I stop
to press my face
into your hair

Hovland, Minnesota

The girls finally tire of their wild dances.
The sun begins to slide behind the pines.

I sit upon a driftwood throne, watch
waves break white against beach rock.

At the far horizon, sky and water cease
their slight division, melding into a single blue.

Meanwhile, my own mirrors, ages nine and five,
seem to grow a little further from me every day.

But on this night they come in close.
We huddle together in a tattered old quilt,

and I tell them tales of Ole Brunes, the first
immigrant fisherman to build in this bay,

the storms he battled, the cows he sailed
up along the coastline from Grand Marais.

Many others since have fished this rich spot
where the Flute Reed flows into Superior.

They also loved daughters, and they watch now
with a jealousy only the dead have earned.

I feel our impermanence like a wild storm
inside my bones, draw the quilt tighter

against the bluster and chill of the fishermen's
breath blowing off the big lake.

Whatever news they're whispering can be dealt
with later. It is nothing the children need to hear.

The most we can hope for

is that the cock that morning
does not crow,

and the turkey buzzards turn
just a moment from
their afternoon spoils
toward the chime of the church bell,

and in the barrooms that night,
the fractured from across
our wide and dusty county
try their hands at redemption
through recollection,
though their words may prove
no more than frail flowers
tattooed across the shoulders
of the dead.

Maybe, if we are lucky,
someone remembers to read
that Raymond Carver poem
or cue up a lonesome
Hank Williams tune.

And then the March moon
sinks off to sleep
in a fallow cornfield.

And dreaming, she mourns
where only the gospel
plow can reach her.

Storm, Rural Missouri

Though the coming rain
announces itself by rustling
the distant corn,
the barns remain immutable
as weathered grey monks.
Without words, they pray
over the dog who sleeps
forever in his soil bed
beside the oranged relic
of a horse-drawn plow.
On rage the blood sugar wars.
The lust for nicotine continues.
The time-crumpled angels
pull on their Carhartt robes
and stand under wide awnings
as lightning unstitches the sky.
Here, every storm is forty nights
from stating the profound.

Colorado

I sit beneath the first sun,
yards from the cautious mule deer,
and name myself by parts:
the right arm of insignificance,
the left eye that also matters not,
the heart about which
no words need be said.
The mule deer grows easier
with each new erasure
until he finally moves
near enough to touch.
But too late—I have receded
into the mountain crags,
turned memory like morning fog.

Photographs

The Work Glove

Tiny Tilted Cross

Sunlight on the Tracks

Harvested

Among the Wildflowers

Reclamation Project

Barn, First Snow

The Abandoned Silo

The Corn Crib

Uneven Track

Tenor Guitar, Barn Wood Loft

No Trespassing

The Windmill

For Sale #3

About the Author

Justin Hamm's books are *Midwestern,* a series of photographs; and two poetry collections, *American Ephemeral* and *Lessons in Ruin.* His poems, stories, photographs, and reviews have appeared in *Nimrod, The Midwest Quarterly, Sugar House Review, Pittsburgh Poetry Review,* and a host of other publications. Recent work has also been selected for *New Poetry from the Midwest* (New American Press) and the Stanley Hanks Memorial Poetry Prize from the St. Louis Poetry Center. Justin's photographs have hung in the Art House Gallery in Fulton, Missouri and have earned a twelve-page, full-color feature in *San Pedro River Review* and the Inkslinger Award from *Buffalo Almanack.* His first solo exhibition took place in the fall of 2017 in Columbia, Missouri; further exhibitions are scheduled for the Normal Public Library in Normal, Illinois; the Mississippi River Gallery in Hannibal, Missouri; and Presser Performing Arts Center in Mexico, Missouri.

www.ingramcontent.com/pod-product-compliance
Lightning Source LLC
Chambersburg PA
CBHW041527090426

42736CB00036B/223